Fire and Rain

*A Cry for Revival
in a Troubled Land*

Dr. Dalen Garris

Copyright © 2018 by Dalen Garris

Cover Art by Christy Pliler

Published by Revivalfire Ministries

ISBN 13:0999469487
ISBN 10: 9780999469484

All rights reserved.
No part of this book may be used or reproduced in any manner whatsoever, without written permission, except in the case of brief quotations embodied in critical articles and reviews, as provided by U.S. Copyright Law.

For information, address
dale@revivalfire.org

Printed in the United States of America

DEDICATION

This is dedicated to the heroes that I have found in both Rwanda and Burundi who know that revival is the only thing that will heal their land and bring them true peace. May God bless your faith and dedication to reuniting both your peoples in Christ.

O Zion, that bringest good tidings, get thee up into the high mountain; O Jerusalem, that bringest good tidings, lift up thy voice with strength; lift it up, be not afraid; say unto the cities of Judah, Behold your God!

(Isa 40:9)

TABLE OF CONTENTS

Chapter 1   A Wind in Rwanda 1

Chapter 2   Rwanda's Cry 4

Chapter 3   Up in the Hills of Rwanda 6

Chapter 4   Three Days in Muhanga 9

Chapter 5   Zero to 60 in Two Services 12

Chapter 6   Where is the Healing Switch? 14

Chapter 7   Breaking a Wall of Ice 16

Chapter 8   The Doorway to Revival 19

Chapter 9   Athens 22

Chapter 10   Kabunga 25

Chapter 11   Ruikira 27

Chapter 12   A Busy Week 30

Chapter 13   Gahini, Birthplace of Revival 33

Chapter 14   Baptism in Rwanda 36

Chapter 15   Mission's End in Rwanda 38

Chapter 16   Out of Rwanda; Into Burundi 41

Chapter 17   Bujumbura 43

Chapter 18   Alexander the Coppersmith 45

Chapter 19   French Restaurant 48

Chapter 20   Like a Fire 50

Chapter 21	A Rainy Day in Burundi	53
Chapter 22	A Day of Encouragement	56
Chapter 23	The Choice of Faith	59
Chapter 24	Small Things	61
Chapter 25	The Evening Balcony	63
Chapter 26	Finishing Up in Gitegi	65
Chapter 27	Breaking Out in Gitegi	67
Chapter 28	Leaving Burundi	69
Chapter 29	Final Results	73
Epilogue:	Report on the Rwanda and Burundi Mission	77
ABOUT THE AUTHOR		81

CHAPTER 1
A WIND IN RWANDA

It was evening when I got off the plane in Kigali and walked across the tarmac to the terminal. The weather here is gorgeous and the temperature is perfect!

As soon as I stepped outside, I could feel the scent of that gentle Africa breeze in the air. I'm not sure what it is or why, but each of the sub-Saharan countries that I have visited have their own distinct exotic scent – similar but slightly unique to each land. As I emerged from the plane, it was as if the land was welcoming me back. I felt at home.

Tomorrow morning, I will catch up on my jet lag and will slowly emerge from the hotel room later on to meet the General Manager of Restore FM, a major radio station in Rwanda. We are starting a 30-minute broadcast in Rwanda, twice a week every Monday and Friday for the next year, and I need to give him the DVD that has the broadcasts on it. As it turns out, he is a good friend of one of my hosts, Pastor Isaiah. Small world.

I will be preaching for three days in a church that is upcountry before coming back to Kigali to launch the "Gideon Generation Movement". University students are coming in from all over the country to be here for this. This movement started at a lunchtime meeting of college students in northern Rwanda when I challenged them to become the Gideon generation and to rise up to answer the call of God that was upon them. I left, not knowing what, if anything, would happen. It has exploded and is about to spill out like a fire into all the rest of the country. I have no idea what I will find when I meet with them at this national conference next week, but it is distinctly in the hands of God.

Lately, I have been reading about the great revivals in Wales, Azusa Street and the Hebrides Islands. I am impressed with the amount and intensity of prayer that preceded each of them – men and women travailing for hours and days under an intense burden of prayer for years. It's not just the length of prayer, which would burden them all night long in many cases, but the depth of travail and the intensity of their souls. Groaning under the burden, they would cry out from the depths of their hearts for God to save souls and revive the Church again. Sounds exactly like what we need in Africa.

We in the West do not pray like that anymore. Not only do we not know how to, we don't even know we are supposed to! Where are the intercessors that would battle their way to the Throne of God all night long, crying out at the top of their lungs, wrestling with the powers of the heavens until the Spirit of God would break forth in victory like the sun shining through the clouds after a storm? Where are the Prayer Meetings at church where the saints would gather to wage war on the spiritual darkness around them, crying out for souls to be saved – and stay there all night long? Where is the yearning down deep in our souls that would drive us to our knees in travailing prayer until we secured the answer from God?

Victories only come after battles, but it appears that we have lost our will to fight. How can we expect a great move of God if we have forgotten how to pray? When we find the strength to lift our voices to God and contend all the way through until we reach the Throne of God, we then release Him to move. Until then, His hands are tied. This is not about God, but about the preparations of our own hearts so we can receive that which He has for us.

Fallow ground is too hard to receive seed. It must first be broken up and watered with the tears of repentance before it is prepared to bring forth the harvest. So our hearts must be broken before God can move amongst us in His great power. It begins with His Word – a hammer which breaks the rock in pieces. It will not be our good works or good intentions that will be the catalyst that brings revival, but the power of the Word of God that works in us to bring us to that place of Holy Ghost conviction. And then, all the glory will go to God. And that's when He can begin to move.

"But we have this treasure in earthen vessels, that the excellency of the power may be of God, and not of us."
(2nd Corinthians 4:7)

CHAPTER 2
RWANDA'S CRY

It is impossible to think or talk about Rwanda without considering the Genocide that still hovers over them like a cloud in the background. On the surface, all seems to be well as they make huge efforts to bury the genocide that destroyed them. Visiting the memorials that they have constructed testifies to those efforts. It is a chilling experience as you walk through the halls that cry for the one million innocents who were slaughtered by their friends and neighbors in 100 days – a bloodbath of horror like nothing you have ever seen. These memorials have been built not only to honor the dead and remember the tragedy, but also to bring healing to Rwanda's devastated soul so that this will never happen again.

These are peaceful, humble people, many of whom are active Christians, and there are witnesses to the Christian faith everywhere. Shout out a "Praise the Lord!" in public, and you will get an "Amen!" from someone standing nearby. So why would the Lord send me to a place that has such an obvious covering of Christianity?

I believe that the appearance on the outside does not accurately reflect the dark recesses of their souls. To the casual observer, Christianity is spread almost everywhere here, but as you begin to plumb the depths of their souls, you find a shell that covers the pain and bitterness that is too deep to describe.

How can such pain begin to be healed which has cut them so deeply? This is not a place for psychologists and sociologists to ply their theoretical therapies. It will not work here – the pain is too deep. Revenge and hatred are strong emotions that are almost impossible to control.

What is needed here is not more therapy; not even more "church". What is needed here is a supernatural outpouring of the Spirit of God in the form of a true Holy Ghost revival – the kind that is real. Only the power of such an outpouring can heal this society.

The message of revival that I bring, however, is not an easy one. True revival is not about feeling good or seeing miracles, or having a wonderful time in church -- it is about winning the lost. There is a high price of a broken, crucified walk that must be paid to bring such a revival.

Many turn from that message because they are looking for the blessings to cover their pain. Others, however, understand the price and the need, and they are excited to hear a message that breaks through the cloud of a worldly, easy Gospel. They know there is a price to pay and that this is the only hope for their country. Sowing mercy on others brings healing to ourselves. It is to those people that I am sent. They are the ones who will carry the torch.

It will not be easy. Satan is determined to destroy these people, but I believe God has a plan and He will make a way for the Truth to triumph over the darkness in Rwanda.

CHAPTER 3
UP IN THE HILLS OF RWANDA

"Oh that thou wouldest rend the heavens, that thou wouldest come down, that the mountains might flow down at thy presence,

As when the melting fire burneth, the fire causeth the waters to boil, to make thy name known to thine adversaries, that the nations may tremble at thy presence!" (Isaiah 64:1-2)

Our first set of meetings is in Muhanga, an hour's drive from Kigali, the capital of Rwanda. I have no idea what to expect – sometimes it will be an incredible surprise; sometimes it is just warm-up for the rest of the campaign. Most of the bigger outpourings of the Holy Spirit seem to happen in the small villages out in the country, so I don't mind driving an hour to minister to God's hungry children out here. They do more for me than I do for them.

They say that Muhanga is where everything starts in Rwanda, including the Genocide. I have been asked to come here because the cold wall of unforgiveness still grips the hearts of these people. That is not surprising considering the extreme horrors that took place. My host tells me that they have asked me to come to Muhanga for two reasons: they need revival here desperately because of the spirit of unforgiveness that lingers, and because it is in Muhanga that everything starts in Rwanda.

All that may be well and true, but do they want revival is

the question I ask. If they are not willing to let go of the old hatreds and passions, there's not much I can do. I don't have anything special to offer other than the message that God has given me. The spark of revival has to happen between the hearts of people who are desperate for God and the throne of His mercy. For some reason, I am not feeling the usual excitement inside me that pumps me up to drive into each campaign. Maybe it's from lack of sleep, maybe I'm not tanked up enough on reading and prayer, or maybe there is a cold layer of ice in the hearts of these people that is shutting out God. Whatever it is, I was not expecting what came next.

Instead of a little country church where a couple dozen poor people are waiting for me, I walk into a large building where over 250 people start cheering and clapping as I enter. I am thoroughly amazed. Here is hope, because it is not for me that they are cheering, but it is for the promise of revival. I may not have a "feel" for what the message will be yet, but God has to feed His people. It will come.

The evening service is even more incredible. Now there are over 700 people in this place, all singing and praising God at the top of their lungs. Again, as I walk in, they start cheering. It is deafening. How can God not hear? I have decided to bring the message from the Book of Joel and show them the prophesies of the coming great revival first before launching into the usual series of messages about how badly the Church in the last days would need a true, Holy Ghost revival. I am told that they normally win about 300 souls every month, so how can I reprove them about not winning souls? These people are already on the road to revival, so what is it that I can give them?

But there is still something missing here. I can feel it but I don't know what it is. As the message pours out of me for the next hour and a half, I get this sense of people stuck inside a bucket, peering over the edge at me. They want what I am telling them about, but they are stuck in something that keeps them from being free. I don't know what it is yet, but this will not be the usual set of messages that I bring. I will have to be totally yielded to the Spirit to navigate these waters so that God can break through whatever this barrier is in their hearts.

And right now, I don't feel very yielded or up to the task. But then, when am I ever? I just have to close my eyes and step off the cliff, and let God do what He is going to do.

Rend the heavens, O God, and let the mountains of Rwanda flow down at Thy presence!

CHAPTER 4
THREE DAYS IN MUHANGA

This is the second day here in Muhanga and for this afternoon's service, we are being taken to a different church that we are assured is nearby. Uh huh. Nearby … as in I-don't-know-how-many miles down rutted mountain roads, over hills, and around valleys? At one point we had to get out and walk because the car couldn't make it up the hill with us in it.

I spotted the church on top of a hill and it looked bigger than what I was expecting. I was expecting the usual 20 x 50 church with a corrugated roof, wooden posts, dirt floor and no walls, but this was actually a real building … and it was pretty big. As we pulled into the yard, dozens of people started yelling and waving their arms in the air. I was a little spooked at first, but then I realized they were welcoming us! But that didn't prepare me for when I walked into the church.

Inside this church was close to 800 to 1,000 people packed like sardines from front to back, and as we walked in, the whole place exploded! I have never seen anything like it! If you have never heard a thousand people cheering at the top of their lungs inside a crowded building, let me tell you it is deafening!

Services were great. They even got me to get up and take part in a tribal dance. (I think Brother Noah caught it on video.) As usual, I poured out my heart for an hour or so to tell them as much as I could about revival. I had to squeeze 6 to 10 messages into this one service because I would not be coming back, so I gave it all I had. Somewhere around the middle, I could feel that rolling breeze of the Holy Spirit take over and we were sailing! The people were so excited that you couldn't keep them sitting down. When I gave an altar call, they came from everywhere. Over forty souls got saved.

Besides the crowd inside, there were a hundred or so people waiting outside because there was no room inside. They stood piled up by the windows, leaning in to hear the Word of God. When I came out to leave, they crowded around me, shaking my hand, touching me, or just plain staring wide-eyed at me. Kids thronged me and mothers pushed through with their babies for me to lay my hands on each one and bless them before I left. It really grabs your heart to see these simple folk reaching out in such desperation for God to touch them and leave a blessing in their hard and poor existence.

We headed to the regular evening service and experienced the same thing there. Between 700 and 800 souls filled the place to hear a message about revival. These were not the curious or bored looking for some entertainment. Neither were they coming because they thought they were supposed to. This church is a long walk from the main town, so if you are planning on coming, you have to be serious about it. The power went off a few times, so the lights went out and the microphone went dead, but no one ever budged. I had to get down off the pulpit and shout the message to them until my throat was sore, but thirty souls got saved there. That makes 70 for the day.

On the surface, everything seems good – the churches are excited, they understand there is a price for revival, and they hang on every word I speak – but something is wrong. It's as if there is a wall of ice as a barrier that blocks the depths of their hearts from opening up to God. I feel like I am preaching all around the issue but not getting to the heart of it. I had this same feeling last year when I preached in

Rwanda.

    Before I bring forth another message here, I have to find out what is wrong otherwise everything that I am doing here is in vain, maybe even counterproductive. In order for any true revival to take hold, there has to be a breaking deep in the hearts of the people. To bend but not break will end up giving a church a false sense of security, thinking that they are right with God, but never able to completely surrender in broken-hearted repentance. And no revival comes without repentance. Without it, all you have is a very nice church ... but you won't have revival.

CHAPTER 5
ZERO TO 60 IN TWO SERVICES

After yesterday's services, I felt a little cloudy. More like dull and uninspired. Yeah, the services were okay, but I only have three days to bring these people to a place of broken repentance before God, bust open the windows of their faith, and ignite a fire in their church that will change their lives and the lives of everyone around them forever. In three days. Good services ain't gonna make it. You need supernatural, Hell-breaking, Holy Ghost-filled services for that. And that is not what we had yesterday. Oh well. One day down; two to go.

But today ... oh boy, today was a different story!

It was all because of my jet lag. At 3:30 AM, I am wide awake and there is no going back to sleep because my body's time clock is still 8 hours off. Okay, so what do you do with 6 hours on your hands and nothing to do? You read and pray. Since I came out of yesterday's services like I was wandering around in a cloud with no clear grip on anything, I might as well do like it says in Job --

"Hast thou commanded the morning since thy days; and caused the dayspring to know his place; that it might take hold of the ends of the earth, that the wicked might be shaken out of it?" (Job 38:12,13)

I got up and prayed like the old fashioned Revivalists used to do. I commanded the morning, and took hold of the dayspring to shake the wicked out of the Earth. Yeah, it was that good. It took a while to get it, and I wasn't sure what I had, but once I did, I knew I had a hold on something from God and He would bring it forth.

Somewhere in that first few minutes I had them. Yesterday, they paid attention, but I never really had them – I mean, HAD them. But today they were locked in. Don't ask me how or why because I have no idea. I don't know what did it, but something broke, and after that we were flying. Never, ever underestimate the power of prayer!

I thought that first service was great. Silly me. The first service was just preparation for the second service. That is when the skies broke wide open ... and stayed open ... for hours. They were still going when I left for the hotel. And I have another day to go yet!

You know, sometimes I feel like I'm wandering around in a cloud and I don't know what I'm doing. Well, actually, that's true – I don't know what I am doing. But that is the strength of my ministry. I may have no idea what I'm doing, but I know the One who does.

Never underestimate the power of prayer.

CHAPTER 6
WHERE IS THE HEALING SWITCH?

I told you about the services on Day 2 in Rwanda. Day 3 was also good, but it was all rolled into one 5-hour service that ended with an hour-long healing line.

This wasn't like healing lines I've had before where you can feel the oil flowing from the Throne and everyone who comes forward gets healed. During times like that, you can actually feel the Anointing flow. It's almost like you are floating – not so much that you can't stand up or anything, but enough that you can feel it. This was not one of those times. I didn't feel anything except for a few individual exceptions. And I'm not so sure that everyone got healed. As a matter of fact, there were several who did not get healed. Why is that?

I know that some people have the Gift of Healing and some do not. I must not have it because I can't turn it on when I need it. I have absolutely no control over when it works and when it doesn't. I can barely pray over some people, and bang, they are healed. Then I pray my guts over someone else and twist my soul in passion for God to heal them, but nothing happens. Is there a method to this? Where is the switch that I'm supposed to turn on? How does this thing work, anyway?

I thought that maybe it was the way I prayed. Are you supposed to pray with the authority that Jesus gave you to go forth and heal the sick, or do you retract humbly before God to beseech Him for healing because it is God who has the power, not you? I tried both and I can't tell if either way actually makes a difference.

Is it the place or the people? Are they not ready, or not open, or not something else? Maybe they don't read the Bible enough so they don't have enough faith to receive healing? Or maybe it's just me. Maybe I'm the one who is not reading enough and doesn't have enough faith. Today I'm lit up and on fire, but tomorrow I'm just flat. I don't know, but all those excuses sound a little thin. If we had some kind of ON switch we could turn on, we'd be running around all over the place healing the sick and raising the dead, waving our hands in the hospitals to empty the place out, standing outside Funeral Parlors to pop them out of the caskets as soon as they put them in them. No, I don't think that's the way it's supposed to be.

Maybe there is no specific reason that you can nail down and analyze. Maybe you just have to trust God and let Him worry about the details. These people are, after all, His sheep, not yours.

I believe that it may not be about healing at all, but about an entirely different dynamic that is at work here. The Gift of Healing might just be a tool that God uses to bring a higher purpose to light through the power of the Gospel. It is not miracles, after all, that can transform a human soul, but only the power of the Word of God that can give you Eternal Life. Maybe that's what it is all about.

CHAPTER 7
BREAKING A WALL OF ICE

I've been praying hard for God to show me what is the problem that I am facing here in Rwanda. The normal set of messages that I bring just will not work here. It's as if the Lord refuses to allow it. So I can feel myself wandering around trying to grab an anchor for the message. Something is wrong, and this morning the Lord opened it up to me.

Unforgiveness is killing these people. Not just physically, but spiritually. In 1994, Genocide stormed through Rwanda when the Hutus slaughtered one million Tutsi's in 100 days. The hatred and bitterness for the horrible acts of barbaric butchery is too deep to describe in words, and the intense pain has created a wall of ice that blocks the bottom of their hearts. On the surface, all is well, but down deep there are raw wounds that have not healed. I understand the pain – my God, I have no idea what I would have been like had it been me — nevertheless, there cannot be any revival here until this wall of unforgiveness is broken down.

The hatred between Tutsies and Hutus is still raging. Last night, someone threw a grenade into a group of people here in town, killing at least two and wounding several others. It seems that great moves of God are birthed out of pain and suffering. Perhaps that is the only way God can cut through the outer layers of fat and grease that smothers our hearts to touch the real pathos of our souls. If that is so, then that explains the intense hunger that these people have for the Gospel.

The level of excitement here is incredible! Hundreds pour into whatever church I am in, having walked for miles to get there, just to soak up anything and everything I can deliver. One hundred souls have been saved in the last two days alone. How wonderful! And yet, with all this desperate hunger and crying out to God, that wall of unforgiveness blocks the innermost recesses of their hearts and closes them off from God. It's killing them.

This afternoon, I met with about 200 pastors and leaders and brought them through the Lord's Prayer. The entire ending of that prayer is about forgiving those who have trespassed against us. If we cannot forgive others, then neither can the Lord forgive us. There are no exceptions, no level of degrees, no mitigating circumstances, and no excuses. Pretty severe. I see no way around it. These people have everything else that would drive them into a great move of God here, but this root of bitterness and hatred eradicates everything. There can be no revival with unforgiveness.

The pastors agree that this pain lies over the people like a dark shroud, but they do not know what to do about it. I asked them if they would like to have an altar call. Deliverance for others must begin with ourselves before we can minister it to others.

There is no feeling like seeing the bursting forth of weeping and tears from broken hearts at the altar of God. I know of no other solution. There is no 10-Step Plan to complete deliverance and victory; no DVD, program, or book that can do this. Flesh cannot win spiritual battles. Only God can do this.

The tragedy of Rwanda is that, after all the horrors of Genocide that they have suffered, this wall of unforgiveness would keep them back from the one thing that can dissolve all the pain and torment and set them free – a true, Heaven-sent, God-fearing, soul-saving, Holy Ghost revival.

Dear God, give me the power to deliver your Word as a hammer that will break this rock in pieces and set them free! As great as the darkness is that has afflicted these people, let your power be ever so much greater. Oh God, send revival!

CHAPTER 8
THE DOORWAY TO REVIVAL

True to human nature, we like to view the idea of revival as a time of great rejoicing, singing and dancing, and an explosion of the joy of the Lord. But the fact of the matter is that for every revival, both Biblical and in history, the doorway to revival is filled with the exact opposite.

No revival comes without repentance. Nehemiah knew this as did Daniel. Even after reading in the Word of God about the restoration of Jerusalem (which is a picture of revival), Daniel did not go celebrate with Shadrach, Meshach and Abednego, but instead dropped to his knees in repentance. It was written in the Word of God so it had to come to pass, nevertheless, revival must be preceded by a time of great repentance. Holiness must precede the outpouring of the Holy Ghost.

It is at the Altar of God where we seek the face of God for an entrance into His Spirit. That is the door that leads to revival. But the Altar is not a place of singing and dancing. It is a place of blood, sacrifice, and death! It is the place where the fire falls, but the fire only falls on a blood-soaked dead sacrifice. The desperate cries of Rachael, "Give me children lest I die!", must be the soul-wrenching cry of those who fall to their knees in humble, broken repentance to cry out to God for revival. These prayer warriors and intercessors are the ones who travail through the birth pains to bring forth any move of God. Their cries must reach Heaven. This is not a time for the faint or hesitant – this is a desperate weeping of the soul for the deliverance of God's people. There is no room for defeat or denial – we must have revival lest we die!

How quickly these lessons are overshadowed by more superficial images of a church enjoying a great time of rejoicing and praise! We tend to overlook the things that are unpleasant, and focus on the things that make us happy. We are like children. Proverbs 22:15 says, "Foolishness is bound in the heart of a child, but the rod of correction will drive it far from him." To approach the holy presence of God with a superficial attitude that dismisses the chilling fear of God will never bring revival. If anything, it will drive it far from you.

I preached to a gathering of university students yesterday who spent an hour or so in loud singing and dancing, jumping up and down, waving hands, and shouting the praises of God. It was wonderful … until I brought a message of repentance and the price that God requires for a true and lasting revival. The room quieted to a somber level and much of the crowd began to dissipate. It wasn't fun anymore.

I worried that it might be my fault. Perhaps I was not deep enough in the Spirit, or I had not presented the message correctly, or had done something wrong to change the atmosphere so dramatically. But when we left there, we stopped by another church in the city where I delivered pretty much the same message to several hundred people. What a difference! The hands went up, the voices exploded with enthusiasm, and the prayers broke through the ceiling! It was as if they had been waiting for God to please send someone with this message. They were so desperate for revival that they were ready to pay whatever price was required.

I went back to the college that evening for another session assured that everything would now be different. I was ready to deliver a message of Elijah's challenge. I could feel that tingling feeling up and down my arms that told me I was in the Spirit. But, again, after the singing and dancing was over, they were still not ready to receive a message that pointed them to a broken surrender of repentance, deep prevailing prayer, and a desperate crying out to God. What was the difference between the two places? It wasn't the message – that was the same in both places. It was the hearts.

Unless the fallow ground of our hearts is broken up, it cannot receive the seeds of the harvest. And then that broken ground must be watered with the tears of repentance and weeping. Only then will you see those seeds of the Word of God that have been planted begin to germinate and grow up into a great harvest of souls.

Revival is not about having a great church service or a wonderful time of praise in the Lord. It is about winning souls. That is the reason God sends revival – to revive His Church to rise up to the calling placed upon her to be fruitful and multiply and fill the Earth with fruit. It is the call to true Charity – the giving of yourself out of love, so that souls can be saved. This is the purpose of revival; it is the message of the Cross; it is the great call upon all of us to deny ourselves, pick up our cross, and follow Him. And where did He go? To Calvary to die so that souls could be saved. Including you.

Anything else is a cheap imitation of the Grace of God and will not bear forth fruit.

CHAPTER 9
ATHENS

I know you can't judge long term effects by short term results, but sometimes it's nice to see the end from the beginning ... or at least as you're on your way there. We have planted seeds today, but there's no telling which will grow and bring forth fruit and which will not.

It was another day of contrasts. I spent the night in prayer – not because I'm so spiritual, but because that stupid jet lag woke up again at 2:00 am and I was wide awake. I figured I could do one of two things: either torment myself by lying in the bed for the next few hours trying to go to sleep, or make the assumption that the Lord woke me up to get up and pray. Figuring that I might as well make the most of it, I stayed up to pray. By morning, I was pumped and ready for anything. I felt like my feet were firmly planted on something solid and I had a grip on God and could tackle the challenges of the day with all confidence. Before the day was out, I was going to need that confidence.

It was Sunday and the morning service was at a fairly large church in Kigali. Normally, this is their day for healing services, but the pastor had been told that if he let us bring a message about revival, his congregation would be blessed. He took a chance and let me come.

This was a wonderful church. You could feel that warm feeling in the air as soon as you walked in. The joy of the Lord was in this place. If I lived in Kilgali, this is where I would want to go to church. As I took the pulpit, I could feel the Spirit begin to flow. Oh, this was going to be a great service!

I have often said that my job is simply to show up. I don't control the message or the Spirit that brings it, and I don't control the hearts of the people to receive it. I just show up. Granted, I had better be in the Spirit – read up, prayed up, and fasted up – so that I can be a yielded vessel for God to control. Our flesh has to be crucified for the Spirit to work freely through us. That's my job, but all the rest is up to Him. I'm just there to be a mouthpiece. When things are open and flowing, it is because the hearts of the people are open to receive from God. Conversely, when the message is not flowing, something is blocking that connection between them. As in Fluid Dynamics, the receiving end has to be open to enable the flow.

This church was wide open. The Spirit of God touched some souls there like they had not experienced before. You know you've hit the bullseye when people tell you that the reason God sent you to Africa was specifically for them. If you are operating under the Anointing, that happens all the time. When God is anointing the message, He is able to reach out to touch the innermost places of their hearts. He is a personal God.

What we experienced at the University that afternoon, however, was just the opposite. We had gone to great lengths and expense to bus these kids in and give them the *Four Steps to Revival* booklets because they had said they wanted to launch the Gideon Generation Movement. Once the service had started, however, it was as if something was blocking the flow of the Spirit. We just could not punch through the wall of impassive faces that stared back at us. I felt like Paul in Athens. Intelligence and education can be great liabilities because they promote the cerebral over the spiritual and make you think that you are smarter than what you really are. What a tough crowd!

What was different? All covenants with God are predicated on humility. The Tree of Knowledge offers you a fruit that is desired to make you wise in your carnal mind, but the Tree of Life requires you to surrender all to God. In order to enter into a covenant with God to send revival, we must come to a place of repentance before God so that He can take over the Church. That will not happen through logic or intelligence but only through a broken heart. Unless we realize the vast difference between the corruption of flesh and the holiness of God, we can never truly come to a place of repentance and break before the Altar of God. And until that happens, God cannot use you.

Both Noah and myself prayed over them and cried out to God to pry open their hearts and give them true understanding. They have heard a message that they have not heard before in that revival is not about singing and dancing but that there is a price to pay for revival. We have handed out about 1,000 booklets that have the message that we have been bringing all over Africa. Our prayer is that they will read it and, like the Bereans, will search the Scriptures and see if these things are true.

My job is to show up. It is God's job to take it from there.

CHAPTER 10
KABUNGA

We are now in Kabunga, Rwanda, a small town that has the only hotel for miles. The place is clean and tidy and fairly comfortable except for the water. You have to be ready to catch it when its running, which apparently is only for a short while around 6:00 am. After that, it's a slow dribble into a plastic tub from which you then scoop it out to pour over yourself for a shower. I guess you might say that it's part of the adventure.

I preached at this same church last year, but the pastor had been out of the country. He has been waiting for me to come back ever since. The Lord energized his congregation after I had left and turned it into a soul-winning church. They have taken the message to the streets, the hospitals, and anywhere they could to witness to the lost and his church has grown significantly. And this pastor wants more.

Lately, the Lord has been trying to teach me the lesson of unreserved trust. I got this strong feeling not to prepare my message for this afternoon. While I never prepare my messages in a typical sense, I do like to have an idea of which direction I am going. But not this time. It is difficult to sit there and not allow your mind to search out different passages that I might use or different subjects to follow. But it was like trying to grab hold of a mist.

Just before I got up to go to the pulpit, I burst out with, "You lead, Lord, and I will follow". Immediately, the scripture about Abraham in Hebrews 11 flashed through my head. Another message about revival that I had never before considered! I wasn't sure where we were going with this, but we were going somewhere! I jumped up with a renewed exuberance and headed for the pulpit.

Fire ran up and down that church that night as the message poured out of me. I'm sure glad I didn't try to figure out what I was going to say because I'd have never figured this one out. I watched as God began to move amongst the congregation and break through to their hearts. Even the pastor, who normally is a very sedate, composed person, was jumping up and down in excitement on top of his chair, and as the services were ending, he was dancing along with everyone else in a Spirit-led celebration which lasted for I don't know how long. And this came from a message of challenge and repentance, not of blessing and false promises! Go figure.

Another 20 souls got saved at the end of the service. That makes well over 400 souls since we began two weeks ago. These souls see the fire of God running in services and they want to be part of it.

Victory comes when you surrender to God. And learning how to let go and trust Him is part of that surrender. When you do that, you untie the hands of God so He can take over and do the miraculous.

My friend Barry put it well: it is like driving a stage coach at breakneck speed down a winding mountain road in the middle of the night in a pouring rain with a sheer drop-off just inches to your side ... and you just throw the reins to the horses!

It takes courage to trust the Lord to that degree. It also takes a hope that is birthed out of a desperation for something more than just "church as usual".

We had a taste of that tonight.

CHAPTER 11
RUIKIRA

Our next stop is at a little village called Rukira in eastern Rwanda. Leaving the town of Kabunga, we have to head out on some dirt roads over the hills, through the valley, and up the next mountain to get there. There are no hotels out here, so we will have to commute from Kabunga for three days. The brothers are telling me that there is going to be a thousand people there. Uh huh. A thousand, did you say? Typically in Africa, whenever you are told one thing, you can expect something else, so I'm figuring that maybe 50 people will show up.

I was wrong. There were somewhere between 3,000 to 4,000 people waiting for us.

Coming with us was Theo, a celebrity friend of my partner here, Pastor Isaiah. Both of them are very popular singers and their songs can be heard on the radio throughout Rwanda. Theo is so popular that wherever we stopped, people would throng him. I wouldn't say he was quite like Elvis, but he was definitely a celebrity. So between Theo and Isaiah, we had a draw that brought people from miles and miles around. Fine with me. I'll use whatever I can to bring the message to as many people as I can.

Needless to say, we had a great time. Besides all the singing and rejoicing which could be heard from miles away, we had an altar call to which so many people responded that I couldn't count them -- maybe 150 to 200? Calling souls down to the altar is not hard to do. All you have to do is ask and they will come. When you assume everyone is saved just because they came to church, your lack of courage spurns the souls who desperately need more than just a Sunday afternoon service.

The next day, I spoke to the church and the Lord stopped me from delivering any message about revival until sin had been dealt with in the church. At times like these, you have to throw out whatever you think you're supposed to do or say and trust the Lord to speak through you. Let me tell you, that is not always easy, but if you can just let go, the results are ... well ... supernatural. If you want to see God move, you have to let Him have His way. If you don't, well, you're on your own. Good luck with that.

The great sin in this place has to do with unforgiveness. If you cannot forgive others, God cannot forgive you, and subsequently, there can be no revival as long as this sin blocks the path. This area was tortured with the Genocide in 1994 and the bitterness runs deep. They may have covered it up on the outside, but it has been festering away down in the bottom of their hearts. On the surface, these people may have been all good Christians; inside they are like dead men's graves.

I felt the Lord lead me to stop the message and call them to repentance instead. For the next half hour, it was like a dam had burst! There was no stopping it once their hearts broke. Weeping and crying out to God in tortured desperation, and grasping the Throne of God for mercy, the whole congregation was swept along by a mighty flood of repentance. All Noah, Isaiah, and I could do was just stand there and let them go. We stood there for 45 minutes. (I actually timed it.) Anytime that we attempted to regain control of the service, they just rolled right over us while they poured out their hearts to God.

What a cleansing! What a refreshing in the Lord! You could feel a dark burden lift off the church as they were set free. As we ended the service, there was a rejoicing in the Spirit that had been a long time in coming. People were hugging, laughing and crying with each other as a great joy filled the place. Something great has just taken place here that will affect the future of this whole area. The sin has been washed away and the victory has come.

Surrendering to God implies trust. Not only as trust in what God can do, but also that He will use you if you just let Him. Reliance on organization, planning, and figuring out every detail is just a sign of a lack of your total trust upon the Spirit of God to take over. When you completely surrender to His will, miracles happen.

And when they do, all the glory will go to God.

CHAPTER 12
A BUSY WEEK

It has been an exhausting week. If I didn't feel an obligation to tell you all about the things that have happened, I would probably just roll over and go to sleep, but I feel these events that are happening here are important because they are a precursor to the great move of God that is coming in these last days.

Am I a hopeless optimist? I don't believe so. I am too much of an analyst for that. I can see what is coming by what is written in the Word, and I can see that the things that are transpiring right now fit perfectly into what has to be His plan. When you can add up the numbers, the answers will always make sense.

When I first started coming to Africa in 2004, I had no idea why I was here, what I was doing, or where this all was going. I have always believed in the great end time revival spoken about in Joel, Isaiah, and hinted at in other prophets, but could never pin a timestamp on it other than that it would be just before the Day of the Lord. The Lord showed me, however, that that day was coming up pretty quick, even in our generation.

The mission became focused when the Lord showed me a vision while I was in Nairobi. I saw of a field of wheat before me that stretched from Kenya to Nigeria. The wheat was so dry and brittle that it had turned white. I watched myself step into that field, strike a match, and drop it into the grass. As the field of grass exploded into flame, the Lord spoke to me that that was His people in Kenya.

Okay, I'm not stupid. I get it now. Go preach revival to Africa and start the fire. So I started coming to Africa and kept on coming. Fifteen years later, I would not have expected to still be coming, but here I am still preaching the same message -- modified and evolved somewhat, but basically with the same thrust.

So when is this Great Africa Revival going to show up? I don't know, but does it really matter? I mean, after all, I can't just snap my fingers and command the Heavens. I have to wait just like everybody else ... and keep striking matches.

But lately, I've noticed that the pace is speeding up. Last year was pretty intense, but this year has been even more so. I'm preaching to more places and to wider audiences than ever. The crowds are getting bigger and more people are recognizing the power in this message. More people are getting saved and healed, and more churches are getting fired up than ever before. And I am running at a harder pace than ever ... and boy, do I feel it.

Towards the end of this week, I was so worn out that I was beginning to feel like a block of stone -- a talking robot if you will. I couldn't remember what day it was or what I was about to say. And don't ask me to cross the room and remember what I was going to do! I just kept going, two, three, and four services every day. Keep preaching; keep bringing the message; keep going. I would be in a daze until I stood up behind the pulpit, and then, I'm telling you, the Spirit would come down and I would wake up and all that mind-numbing fog would dissipate like smoke.

I don't know how much longer the Lord will have me punching out this message. Will I get too old or sick? Will people get tired of supporting this ministry? Will God keep pouring out His fire in service after service? Is He going to keep healing people and winning souls? I guess those are not my problems. I just gotta keep going.

I am seeing more and more brothers and sisters picking up the torch and going forth to light more fires. They've heard the message, felt the fire, and have answered the call. The fire is spreading and the pace picking up.

CHAPTER 13
GAHINI, BIRTHPLACE OF REVIVAL

"We struggled through the hours of the night, refusing to take a denial. Had He not promised? And would He not fulfill? Our God is a covenant-keeping God, and He must be true to His covenant arrangement. Did He fail us? Never! Before the morning broke, we saw the enemy retreating, and our wonderful Lamb take the field."

"We had a consciousness of God that created a confidence in our souls which refused to accept defeat."

[Peggy Smith, the 82-year-old blind woman, who along with her 84 year old sister contended in prayer until they had spawned the great Hebrides revival.]

On our way to our last series of services in Rwanda, we drove past Gahini, the place where the East African Revival first broke out in a little round building just off the highway. It was small and unassuming by any standards, and nothing would have suggested anything extraordinary, but this is the place where the heavens first broke wide open and started an outpouring of the Holy Ghost that swept across the Africa.

It was here that a small group of determined prayer warriors took hold of the horns of the altar of God and crashed the gates of Heaven, crying out to God with broken hearts for God to send revival. They gathered in this tiny place and cried and cried and cried out to God to send revival. They were just a handful of simple country folk, but they had the courage to believe God and hold Him to His Word. They refused to let go until He sent revival, and when it came, it broke out like a fire that raged across the continent.

Our generation has forgotten the art of spiritual war. We pray like children in comparison to these old warriors who, like Elijah, knew how to storm the Throne of God. When we hold revival prayer meetings, we do more fellowshipping with each other than serious contending with God. It's because we are not desperate – not like those people in Gahini for whom nothing else mattered. Like Rachael in Genesis 30:1, their cry was, "Give me souls or else I die!" That is the difference between us and them.

Before leaving, we stood in the center of that tiny room and bound together in contending prayer for God to once again send revival to this land, to rend the heavens and come down in the fullness of His power. Break forth like a fire and consume us with your glory! Send revival once again, O God!

We were standing on holy ground – the very place where the fire had broken out years ago. I felt like I was standing at Bethel, the very entrance to Heaven. As we lifted our voices, it felt as if a hole had already been punched into the heavens by the saints that had been here before us, and our prayers shot straight into the Throne Room of God. I knew – absolutely knew – that we were standing right before the God of the whole Earth – right before His Throne! He had heard us and He had answered us. The answer was already on the way. It was such a powerful sensation that I began to laugh and laugh and laugh. We were standing in the Presence of God!

Lightning rarely strikes in the same place twice. This shrine to the East African Revival sits in the middle of a placid Anglican compound on top of a hill overlooking a lake. No one prays there anymore; the ringing cries of the old dedicated warriors are no longer heard through the night. Souls no longer get saved there and the sick no longer come to get healed. There are no shimmers of the Shekinah glory to be seen or songs of revival to be heard. It sits as a silent testament of a former generation who were desperate enough to cry out to God and keep on crying until the heavens broke wide open.

There will be one last great revival before Jesus comes back. I believe it will begin in Africa. Across this continent from Kenya to Nigeria, I hear the echoes of that same desperation that drove those old warriors to the Throne. God can hear them also. It is a unique sound that is unlike any other.

It is the sound of an abundance of rain.

*"And Elijah said unto Ahab, Get thee up, eat and drink;
for there is a sound of abundance of rain."
(1st Kings 18:41)*

CHAPTER 14
BAPTISM IN RWANDA

Well, I baptized 20 people in a rushing, muddy creek in Rwanda today. That old Oak Ridge Boys song kept running through my head, "They baptized Jesse Taylor in Cedar Creek last Sunday". I'm pretty sure Cedar Creek was cleaner than the creek I was in. Think of being waist high in coffee with cream and sugar rushing down a miniature gorge. One lump or two?

I love baptisms. The toughest part in Africa is getting the names right, but they don't care; they're just thrilled to be getting baptized. Laughing, singing, and praising the Lord, we all stood in that creek, plunging under the water. What a blast!

Then we all headed back to the church for a full-blown service. I wasn't expecting all this, but once I was inside the church, there was no getting out for several hours. The place was packed. It would have driven a Fire Marshall here in America crazy. There was no room to squeeze in one more person, but somehow more people would slide their way in anyway, especially once the music started and the dancing began. We were there for hours. What a service!

How different they are from us in the sedate West. They are not worried about the correct or proper way of doing things – they just do them. Instead of being tampered down with inhibitions, they just let loose. Yes, I suppose we all have our different preferences, but I have to tell you, I want to be in Heaven with these guys, whooping' and hollerin', dancing around like mad, and giving myself over to the passions of praise.

They just have more fun. And I plan on having a whole lot of fun when I get to Heaven.

CHAPTER 15
MISSION'S END IN RWANDA

Our mission here in Rwanda has ended. Tomorrow I head for Burundi for the next two weeks of battle. Funny I should put it that way, but that's exactly what it is like – spiritual battle. The struggle is invisible because it all takes place in the Spirit. I would imagine that to someone who is watching from the side, it would seem that nothing is going on at all, but inside there is a churning and a struggling going on that wrestles in a silence that is only broken in prayer.

I have learned a lot while I was here, most of which has to do with trust. Repeatedly, the Lord would deal with me to quit worrying about the message. Just let it go. Quit trying to figure out some kind of direction before you stand up behind the pulpit. Learn to completely trust God and just yield. Surrender … total surrender.

I can feel that voice whispering, "Do you trust Me? Then quit struggling, and let Me do this! These are My people, not yours. It is My message and this is My revival … not yours".

When I allow my mind to release and relax, the Spirit of God flows through the message with an excitement that I could never have duplicated. It's pretty cool to watch God take over. It feels like you jumped into a boat that is being carried along with a raging current, and you are just along for the ride.

Faith that is absolute has never been natural for me. I'm the type of guy that has to be able to figure everything out before I can fully believe in it. It just has to make sense for me to believe ... and the things of God just do not make sense to the carnal mind. Which is precisely why I was such a stone-cold atheist as I was growing up. I have had a lot of supernatural experiences – I have heard the Lord actually speak to me, I have felt the anointing fall so heavily that we were floating in it, I have seen hundreds of miracle healings, including the blind, the deaf, the crippled, paralyzed, and comas. But even with all that, it has been difficult to surrender completely without any reservation, mostly I guess because I haven't actually seen Him in the flesh. So when I would be getting ready to preach a message, I always strove to feel like I had some kind of grip of what the message was about and where it was going before I got up behind the pulpit. And I would be stressed if I didn't. That is, until I opened my mouth and allowed the Lord to take over.

Don't get me wrong. I believe in being completely led by the Spirit and not to be so carnally organized and prepared that God is left out. I make the boast that the strength of my ministry lies in the fact that I have no idea what I am doing. I don't want to know. God is in charge here.

Nevertheless, a couple of weeks ago I had a dream that woke me up with such a clarity of comprehension that it changed everything. Even though I still have not actually seen God with my eyes, I see clearly the evidence of His supernatural presence that is all around me. The reality of this dimension that is just beyond an invisible veil has all of a sudden become a tangible reality that is startlingly clear to me. It's hard to explain, but it's like, after 42 years, I finally get it! I can see it. It makes sense. It has become real. It is the substance of faith.

To yield and fall back into the hands of God and trust Him for everything is now so much easier. The very substance of His presence is real. He's real, He's there, and He is watching ... and He is involved. That's the part that has really changed for me. He is not a passive spectator -- He is involved! Of course He is going to catch me when I jump off the edge of the cliff! When I pray, He answers. When I lay hands on people, they get healed. When I stand up to give a message, He brings the words and anoints them with His Spirit to deal with the hearts of those out there in the congregation. He always has, it's just that now I'm not worrying about it anymore. I am just the guy standing behind the pulpit.

It has made a difference here in Rwanda. I am no longer worried about what God will do – He just does it. Church after church has been transformed, turned in a different direction and set on fire for revival. God is beginning to move amongst His people, healing broken hearts, lifting crushed spirits, inspiring His people with a vision of inspiring brightness that they have never known, and igniting a hope in them that, yes, God has once again visited His people, and revival is on its way.

In all thy ways acknowledge him, and he shall direct thy paths. (Proverbs 3:6)

CHAPTER 16
OUT OF RWANDA;
INTO BURUNDI

What a cool name, Bujumbura, the capital of Burundi, a sister country right next to Rwanda. What a study in contrasts that for all their similarities, they are tribal polar opposites. Rwanda is populated with Tutsies and Burundi with Hutus. The hatred between the two, since the days of the Genocide, is still intense, and yet, like Jacob and Esau, it is as if they are locked together in tandem for some greater cause. It will take a true Holy Ghost revival to unlock the revolving hatred and restore the brotherhood between them.

We left Rwanda with a bang. As we were getting ready to leave, we were asked to speak at a luncheon service for a church with 10,000 members. Only a hundred or so were there, but the message excited them enough for them to ask us to come to a Sunday service when we come back in 3 weeks. I have to admit, the opportunity to bring this message to 10,000 people is intriguing.

Then as we left that church, we were asked to go on Radio Rwanda which reaches the whole country. Talk about open doors! We have known that something important must be going on because of all the spiritual fire we have been going through, so seeing these doors open up is no surprise. I think there is more going on in the spiritual realm for this country than we realize.

But for now, we are in Bujumbura at the New Visions church with Pastor Domitien. Right off the bat, thirty souls got saved in the morning service and another one this evening. Services were a jumping-up-and-down affair, filled with praises and the joy of the Holy Spirit. Nobody wanted to leave. And that is after 3 and 4 hours. Yeah, it was that good.

But again, just like Rwanda, you can feel something going on in the Spirit that is bigger than just some revival services in a little church. I don't know what it is yet, but I can feel the churning. Things are not just being excited; they are being transformed. This is no longer "church as usual", but a shattering of religious faith to light a torch of on-fire, soul-winning, Holy Ghost revival.

If you don't know the difference between the two, then come to Africa. One dose of this kind of power and you will be forever cured of church as you've known it.

CHAPTER 17
BUJUMBURA

Doesn't that name sound exotic? It carries all the expectations of a deeply foreign African enclave in the heart of this distant, mysterious continent.

And so it is. Where Kigali in Rwanda is clean and almost antiseptic in comparison to this bustling, gritty city, Bujumbura seems to possess more of that easy, flowing African soul. Where Rwanda is a controlled society, Burundi is anything but. Rwanda's populace is constantly aware of keeping all the rules, including seat belts and litter, whereas Burundi's asks the question, "What rules?" Kigali is the Park Avenue to Bujumbura's Greenwich Village. Can you tell which one I prefer? Cindy, I'm sure, would love Kigali, but I can let loose in Bujumbura.

There is also a stronger sense of revival stirring here amongst the churches and the university students. They not only want revival, they are poised for it. I do not have to convince them that the price for revival is high – they already know. When I tell them that I am not a nice guy, they laugh because they don't want a "nice guy". They want the truth!

I have been told repeatedly that I am not like all the other Muzumgu preachers from America with their messages of love, peace, blessing, and prosperity. It makes me wonder what we have been telling these people. Are we so interested in trying to show how nice we are that we have filled them with an insipid Pollyanna Gospel in which everything is beautiful and everybody loves everybody as we tiptoe off into the garden of Love? I am not telling them anything unusual –

just the old-time Gospel that our forefathers preached -- repent or perish! So why is this message standing so far out from the crowd of well-wishers and do-gooders that flock here to spread the American Gospel of Prosperity and Love?

They recognize a severe difference, and while they are accommodating, they are not interested in what they see as an American Gospel. They want something real. After the service last night, an old man came up to me and said, "You really don't care what anyone thinks about you, do you?" Nope. There is too much hanging in the balance.

Revival will not come without repentance, and if it won't come here in Africa where they are so hungry for God, it sure won't come in America where we are far too comfortable to stretch our souls into a desperate cry for repentance from our "church as usual" that we clutch so closely to our hearts. I have to bring this message in a clarity of truth, regardless of what anyone thinks of me, so that those who have open hearts that are ready to hearken and receive this message may plant this seed and bring forth a harvest.

Those who prefer a much easier Gospel have a different path and destination.

> *"And he spake many things unto them in parables, saying, Behold, a sower went forth to sow ...*
> *And some fell among thorns ..."*
> (Mat 13:3,7)

CHAPTER 18
ALEXANDER THE COPPERSMITH

"Alexander the coppersmith did me much evil: the Lord reward him according to his works: (2nd Timothy 4:14)

Burundi is a tiny country nestled in the midst of East Africa. Only a few short years ago close to 300,000 people died here in a 12-year civil war, but now it is clean, open and peaceful and a welcome relief from the squalor you find in Kampala and other cities in Africa.

But for such a small country, I had an incredible amount of resistance and trouble when I first came here. It all surrounded one single person who caused so much trouble. And guess who that person was – our host, the guy who invited me there – my own personal Alexander the Coppersmith!

Without hanging out all the dirty laundry, suffice it to say that it was a battle, but we knew we had to work through it, and in the end, we reached dozens of pastors and leaders with a startling message of revival that they had never heard before. They are ignited and ready to turn Burundi ablaze with a new fire that they have been praying for.

There are churches all over the place and probably 85% of the population are practicing Christians – even the President of the country is born again – but there is a serious lack of depth here. They pray like warriors, but they read Bible like children. Many pastors here have only a rudimentary knowledge of the Bible, and others have not even read it all the way through. I had to help one of them today find the Book of Judges because he didn't know where it was.

With that kind of deficiency, there can be no power in the Church … and no revival. Only the Word of God can bring forth revival.

- Without a deep hold on the Word, your faith will be anemic and you will not have the power to raise your prayers past the ceiling. Oh, you can pray loud, but you won't get very high.

- Without the Word of God, any repentance will be superficial at best because it is the Word of God that separates between flesh and spirit to open your heart for Holy Ghost conviction.

- Without knowledge of the Word, how will you know what to tell the new souls what is right and wrong?

- Without a depth in God's Word, how will you recognize the devil when he comes to destroy the church?

- Without the Word of God, there is no power, no wisdom or understanding, no depth, and no strength.

It's as if they have all the pieces except the most important one.

Ah, but once they grasp the importance of reading the Bible, they cannot hold their excitement. This is what they have been waiting for. It's as if they have been sitting in a dark room and someone just ripped open the curtains to let in the bright sunshine of the day. And then it's, "Get outta the way, 'cause here they come!"

I was taken to a church way out in the bush country in northern Burundi. Pastors and people came from miles around to see the white man from America. At the end of the second service, we gave them some oil to pray over their people for revival. They didn't know what to do with the oil because they had never done this before, and stood there looking at us with blank faces. But oh, once they got the idea, it was like pouring out hot fire on dry tinder!

I don't know how long we prayed – first over those who wanted the fire of God in their lives, then the children, then for healing, and who knows what else after that – that place was transformed. The very air changed. There was a feeling of warm wholeness in the air that gave you a feeling of light. (Sorry, but that's the best I can do in trying to describe the feeling).

Miracles took place there. Miracles that so many of the churches in America and Europe have long ago traded for a modern sophistication that has left them like the Church of Laodicea — rich and increased with goods, but not realizing how blind and poor and naked they have become.

Satan knew. He knew that these people were a tinderbox ready for a move of the Holy Spirit if they could just be pointed in the right direction. So he sent Alexander the Coppersmith to do everything he could to stop the move of God.

In the end, however, God will have His way. He did with Paul in Ephesus, and He did with these people in Burundi. But sometimes that means you have to stand in the battle to fight all the way through to claim that victory.

But the victory is always worth it.

CHAPTER 19
FRENCH RESTAURANT

I ate in a French restaurant yesterday here in Bujumbura. Eating in a French restaurant with the menu written in a language you don't understand can be a little disconcerting. You really don't know what you are ordering and can only hope it won't be too weird. It's like a Pentecostal trying to explain what the Baptism of the Holy Ghost is like to a Baptist. You know they aren't going to fully understand the concept, but you hope they can at least get the general idea.

I ordered Lapin, which is rabbit … I hope. That's as close to a rat as I want to get – a rodent with long ears and a short tail. I just hoped they didn't bring out Fried Lapwing Bat or Muskrat Stew. You never know with the French.

And I hate to say this, but guess what? It tasted like chicken! Surprise, surprise. Next time I will order spaghetti.

Revival ministry in Africa is often like that. You don't always know how everything will turn out, but you go ahead with the same message you have been bringing and hope that the results will be good.

Sometimes the whole place ignites; sometimes they all are crying in brokenness; and sometimes they just sit there and stare at you. Go figure.

You could worry yourself sick about the different results (the devil always tells me that it is my fault because I didn't pray hard enough), but the truth is that your job is just to show up. It is God's job to take it from there. It is His anointing, not yours, that will pierce hearts and touch souls.

All you can do is be enough in the Spirit to deliver what He gives you. The results and the timing of their effects are His responsibility.

That takes all the sweat out of it for me. Sure, I have a responsibility to seek His face in deep prayer and to saturate myself in His Word, but that only serves to allow Him to use me as a conduit. He is the one who does the work.

So I ordered the lapin. Not bad, even for chicken.

Bon appetite.

CHAPTER 20
LIKE A FIRE

"Is not my word like as a fire? saith the LORD; and like a hammer that breaketh the rock in pieces?"
  (Jeremiah 23:29)

It is one thing to talk about the Lord and all the things you believe; it is another to see Him move in power right before your eyes, and we saw God move tonight in His unmistakable power.

As we have moved through Rwanda and into Burundi, we have seen some wonderful things. Day after day, God has manifested Himself by showing how powerfully His Spirit can transform a whole church in just one service. It has happened time after time in Rwanda, it continued in Bujumbura, and now we are seeing it happen here in the rural back country of Burundi. We have preached to almost 10,000 people in the past few weeks and few, if any, have escaped being touched by the hand of God.

You can not only see the Spirit of God sweeping through the congregation, you can feel the wind as it blows through it. Even the unsaved can see it, and that's what brings them down to the altar. This is the real thing. It is what you read about in books and stories that happened a hundred years ago. God is really, really alive, and He is showing up here in these services.

We stopped to do a quick review of the past few weeks, and yes, God has electrified every place we have preached in. This is not the kind of services that these people are used to, neither is it what they have learned to expect from other Americans. This is something special.

Tonight was such a night. We are in Ruyigi, Burundi in a small rural church. The place has been packed for the last couple of days, but tonight it was overflowing because word had spread that something special was going on. You have to understand that these people have come from all over because they are starving for something to happen from God. They have been willing to listen to anyone who would promise revival, but have been disappointed every time. They no longer want to hear about how God is going to bless them and how beautiful Jesus is. Please just tell us the truth! How do we get revival? What are we missing? What do we need to do?

The services were exciting yesterday and this morning, but tonight it exploded! By the time I was done, the Spirit was blowing through the church like a hurricane, but when I turned it over to Pastor Noah, it just let loose! I don't know anyone who can pray down the Spirit over a church like Noah can. The church might have been running with their pedal to the metal when I handed it to him, but Noah kicked in the supercharger. When it had finally died down, over seventy people had crashed the altar for forgiveness – not for the type of regular sins that you would expect, but for settling for "church as usual". "Oh God, please forgive us for being so filled with church that we have ignored the call that You have placed upon us to win the lost!"

And THEN we had the altar call and more souls came up to get saved!

How I wish I could do this in America! But I cannot bring this same message there because their hearts are like fallow ground which has not been broken up. As in the Parable of the Sower, fallow ground that is hard and packed cannot receive the seed and bring forth a harvest. The problem with America is that, like the Church of Laodicea, she does not realize how far she has fallen from where she once was, and therefore resists any message to bring her to repentance so that her heart may be broken up. America is not ready for revival.

Not yet. But it is coming. Maybe not the way we would like, but it is coming. God may have to bring America to her knees in desperation to get her to cry out, but that is the mercy of God. He did that with the Children of Israel in Egypt because, after 400 years, they had gotten used to their slavery. To get them to cry out to Him, God rose up a Pharaoh who killed their children. Once they cried out to Him then He delivered them.

He may do the same to us.

CHAPTER 21
A RAINY DAY IN BURUNDI

It's raining this morning. You'd think that would set a somber tone to the day but actually, it feels refreshing, like washing away all the dust from the last few weeks. I don't have any services until 6:00 pm tonight, so I can just sit here and muse and let the day roll along as it lumbers past me. I must be tired.

There are two strong currents pulling on me. One is pulling on my heart to come home. I'm both physically and emotionally drained and desperately miss all my girls. It is at this stage of every trip that I turn into a cranky old man and everything becomes hard. I am so ready to go home.

But the other current pulls on my heart to keep on going - one more church, one more city, one more soul, just a little more … This message works. It is transforming church after church and opening their eyes, not only to what revival is really about, but the price they have to pay to get one. It's as if this is the missing manual; the secret key to unlock the door; the hidden answer to the desperate cry of their hearts. It is hard to turn from them and head off to the comforts of America when they are so hungry for what the Lord has to give them.

Last night, I spoke to a group of university students who had gathered to hear about revival from the white man from America. As I have heard in so many other places, they were expecting a soft message of peace, love and blessings with false promises that never come to pass. But there was hope that just maybe I might be different, so they came. And once we began, they did not want to go home. It was as if they have been clueless for answers about revival and here, at last, were the answers that made sense. All they have heard are messages of blessings and prosperity that they finally realize do not work. So where are the courageous ministers of our past who had the guts to stand up and tell these people the truth and were not worried about what anyone thought? What happened to them? Where did they go?

I hear this all the time – Africans are tired of the message that they hear from the Americans who come here. One pastor told me that he has to be very careful about promoting someone from America because they always carry the same weak message. How sad that the country that once produced great men and women of God whose messages transformed the world and broke the power of darkness now only produces weak and insipid preachers who have nothing but an anemic gospel to offer in its place.

I preach a different message than what they are used to hearing. There is a price to pay for revival and it begins on your knees. My first job is to shatter their illusion of "church" and point them to the altar of deep, broken-hearted repentance. No revival comes until that threshold has been crossed.

Once the word gets out that here is a message with teeth that is accompanied by the power of the Holy Ghost, everything changes. People want to hear the truth, not some Pollyanna Gospel to make them feel good about themselves. And when they hear it, they come.

So you see, as much as I am dying to go home, there is a strong tugging on my heart to keep going – one more church, one more service, one more group of hungry hearts …

But it is almost time to go. Three more services and I am finished here in Burundi. My money is about gone, but thankfully, a church has offered to pay for my hotel and food for the last remaining days I am here in this town. As soon as

I get home, however, I have to turn around and head for Nigeria – a conference at Abuja in March, a series of churches and meetings in Lagos for April, and then a tour of churches, kings, and crusades in the Delta State in August. I dare not stop until Africa is ablaze with revival. It is only then that this same fire will spread around the world and reach America.

CHAPTER 22
A DAY OF ENCOURAGEMENT

"And John calling unto him two of his disciples sent them to Jesus, saying, Art thou he that should come? or look we for another?" (Luke 7:19)

Just a few days ago, I was questioning my whole mission here. I suppose that happens in every Christian's walk once in a while. You know that you have heard from God, you know that the vision that He has placed in your heart is as real as He is – you know all this – but still, there are those times when the reality of the vision seems far away.

Last week, after ministering in Bujumbura, we drove for two hours up into the back country to minister to another church that was no bigger than a 20 x 20 room. There were twelve people there for services. Now, this is not new for me. I am well-known for going to the places where no one else will go – to the little people out in the tiny churches in the villages and in the Bush. But after a while, you begin to wonder if you are just spinning your wheels. Is this really of the Lord or am I just trying to make believe I have some great ministry in Africa? Am I really accomplishing anything out here, or am I simply wasting the finances that hard-working people have sacrificed to send me out here? And of course, that begs the next question, am I betraying those people who supported me by lying to them that I am accomplishing some great thing out here when I am really only spinning a yarn that will amount to nothing?

Can you hear the devil in the background?

Whenever I have hit a low place and cry out for God to send me encouragement, He has always sent it the very next day. Always. So as I was driving to the last of the meetings in this little town, I stared straight up into the sky and laid my heart out before God. "Is this real? Am I doing what You have sent me to do? Am I really laying the groundwork for the Great African Revival? Or am I just a legend in my own mind?"

Needless to say, as I approached the church, I could hear the rejoicing afar off. The place was packed! Inside was crammed with people, and outside they were leaning in through the windows. What a powerful service we had! Who knows what will come out this tiny church that is now set on fire? I am so sorry, Lord, that I even questioned what You were doing. This is how God does it.

But He was not done with me. Today was supposed to be my day off before we head out to the next village. It was supposed to be a day to rest, but that never happened. Before the day began, I was called to go to the TV station because they wanted me to broadcast this message of revival on TV. They gave me an entire hour on Christian TV to preach to all the churches in Burundi. By the time I got back to the hotel, I was told that the head bishop over the Assembly of God churches in Burundi with over 60 churches wanted to meet me. He had been told about this shattering message I have been bringing and he was desperate for revival – TRUE revival – to come to his church also. Stay where you are - he is coming to the hotel. Before he left, another bishop showed up at the hotel. He also had one of the largest churches in Burundi. The President and his wife attend his church. He also had heard of this message that I bring, and he wanted this to come to his church also.

This is the day after I asked God for some encouragement! Not bad for a day off.

My point? Yes, we will go through valleys where we are

immersed in the shadow. Sometimes it is hard to see even a little distance in front of us. Not only do we not know where we are going, we don't know if we are walking in a straight line or going around in circles. God is somewhere out there, but you can't see Him anymore. The vision of where He is taking you has faded, and you wonder if it was ever real. But you keep on walking. Sometimes it is just to place one foot in front of the other with no idea of where you are heading … but you keep on walking.

But He is always right there. Yes, He spoke to you! Yes, He has commissioned you! Yes, you are who He said you are! Yes, the vision is real! And yes, He is planting the seeds of the greatest revival of all time! Did you doubt Him? Did He not call you to this battle? Is He not the God of Victory? And will He not fulfill His Word?

Yes, as it is written in Isaiah, "He has not said unto the seed of Jacob, Seek ye me in vain". God has spoken; He will bring it to pass. Revival is coming. Keep walking!

"And the LORD shall utter his voice before his army: for his camp is very great: for he is strong that executeth his word:" (Joel 2:11)

CHAPTER 23
THE CHOICE OF FAITH

"Now faith is the substance of things hoped for, the evidence of things not seen." (Hebrews 11:1)

Faith is a choice. It is not something that is thrust upon you or presented as a set of choices to pick from. It is something that you have to reach for that lies beyond the grasp of your understanding. You have to choose to believe.

I have always been struck by the passage in the 2nd chapter of 2nd Thessalonians that tells us that God will send strong delusion to those who do not have a love of the truth but have pleasure in unrighteousness. This life, therefore, is a test for our souls. We are eternal creatures created in His likeness, but our choices determine our final destiny. Will we follow our hearts in a path that leads to self-gratification, or will we choose the fear of the Lord? Only we can make that choice.

Faith, then, is not a matter of believing in God because it makes sense. The Gospel does not make sense to the carnal mind – not the unseen existence of another world, not the path we are called to that leads through the sufferings of the Body of Christ, nor the ultimate victory that was won on the Cross. Everything about God is contrary to the world we live in. And yet, He asks us to close our eyes and believe.

Faith is a choice we make that is born out of Hope. We hope in the righteousness of God. We hope that it is all true that there really is a God who is holy, that Truth is supreme, that those who hunger and thirst for righteousness shall be filled, and that, in the final culmination of all things, we will walk on streets of gold. We hope, and we make a choice to believe in hope as did Abraham, and we rejoice in hope of the glory of God.

Faith that is born out of such hope stretches us past our horizons and creates a vision in our hearts to believe God for the impossible, to take us past what we can see, and reach all the way into Eternity.

Faith is the very substance of that righteousness that we hope for because as we reach through the portal of Eternity, we grab hold of the hem of His garment and touch the Throne of God.

CHAPTER 24
SMALL THINGS

God likes small things. Ever notice that? Not only does He stick up for the poor and needy, but He seems to like using little people from little places, nobodies if you will, to do great things. The big shots like Moses, the prince of Egypt, He breaks down and turns them into nobodies before He can use them. How unlike the way we would do things. But then, He is God and He can do it however He wants to.

While we were in the city of Bujumbura, we had some great services in several of the churches there. Some of them were huge – one had 6,000 members – but others were moderate in size. The people there are hungry for revival like everyone else in Africa, but they are a step ahead of most others. They already understand that the modern Gospel which proclaims blessings and wealth for the believer will not fulfill the promises it claims – certainly not the ones for revival. They know and understand that any true revival comes with a high price, and it will take something special from God to give us the power to pay it. They want a message that gets right to the meat of the matter – tell us what we have to do to bring revival.

Prayer groups are beginning to spring up. Christians are binding together to read the Word with each other. Outreaches are stretching out into the communities to witness to the lost and bring them in. They are setting the stage for the next step to revival. The Presence of God that brings the kind of Holy Ghost conviction that crushes people to their knees in repentance is right around the corner. If you ask God for revival, He will bring conviction, and it will burst forth across the entire church. The house has to be cleansed before He can come in.

This is what we find in the city, but up in the back country where the rural countryside tends to have a lower level of sophistication, God seems to move in greater power. The outbursts of God's power that we found in the two towns we ministered to in the back country were far more explosive then what we found in the city. This has been true wherever I have gone.

Why is that? Are country people less encumbered with the demands of society? Are they less "worldly"? Do they have a clearer picture of Eternity because their vision is not cluttered? Is their faith simple because their lives are simple? I don't know, and I am not trying to figure it out. I have enough to worry about.

What I do know, however, is that God uses the weak things of the world to confound the strong and foolish things to confound the wise so that all the glory goes to God. I also realize that He will use anybody that will simply have the courage to believe Him. He used a teen-age shepherd boy to take down a giant and an 80-year old shepherd to take down a mighty king. And, I might add, a jackass to take down a prophet.

He can use you to change the world. Not the guy next to you – you! You just have to have the faith to take Him at His Word and act on it.

CHAPTER 25
THE EVENING BALCONY

Its quiet this evening as I sit on the hotel balcony watching the sun go down. I love how evenings here have that soft way of settling in, almost like a soft cushion of twilight slowly settling down onto the city. For some reason, the evening comes fast at the Equator. As soon as the sun drops over the horizon, it gets dark. Not like in Texas where it stays light for hours after the sun is long gone. Not sure which I like better, but for now, this has a nice, easy feeling.

I miss my girls. Usually it takes at least a month or so before I start getting lonely, but this trip has been hard, so I'm not surprised that this has already become a "head fire" for me this early. Cindy was right; two months is too long. This is the silent price you pay that others don't see.

But I can't complain. Things have been exciting. The churches we were at in Rwanda and Bujumbura have been literally transformed. They will never be the same ... ever. It's as if the glass ceiling over their Christianity has been shattered and they are soaring into the air. Hundreds of souls have been saved in the past week. Not as many supernatural healings so far, but that will come. I don't know why, but the healings seems to come after the mission is going for a while. Who knows? Maybe I have to get warmed up or something before the oil starts flowing. I have no idea how it works.

We've had enormous challenges and problems on this trip right from the start. Maybe that means this will be a great mission. The trouble always starts on the very day that I purchase the airline tickets – always. That's one clue that there is a satanic intelligence behind all these insane things that happen, from software that crashes, machines that break, doorknobs that fall off, water heaters that quit, and things that get broken, stolen, or lost. And of course, it always happens at exactly the worst time, as if all these things that have gone wrong are on a perfectly tuned satanic schedule.

This time, the trouble has extended to those who are working with me. This hasn't happened before. Pastor Noah had his church broken into and all the audio equipment stolen that he was renting. Guess when that happened … yup, the day I bought the tickets. He has to pay a thousand dollars to the guy who rented him the equipment, but he doesn't even have a hundred bucks to his name.

We always find a way to get through these challenges. God provides in a variety of sometimes very unexpected ways. I guess it's all part of the process in growing your faith and trust in an Almighty God who has already promised that He would take care of you. Instead of being an obstacle that would stop us, I have been taught to look at these things as a catalyst that spurs you forward.

The sun is almost gone over the horizon now, and it'll be dark soon. The evening sounds are just starting to come out. Tomorrow, we will start all over in another city, but for now, I'm just soaking in the quiet of the evening as it settles in. It's nice, and it's quiet, but Lord, I sure miss my girls.

CHAPTER 26
FINISHING UP IN GITEGI

Gitegi is a fair sized town in the hills of Burundi. As in most African cities, the streets are cluttered with shoebox storefronts sporting a cacophony of opposing faded colors, peeling paint, and years of grime. There is a running life to the city that seems to thrive on the disharmony of wild matatu drivers, yelling and honking horns, and shouting hawkers trying to sell you cell phone airtime. It starts in the morning and lasts into the evening when the street vendors come out to roast corn and fry up chapati, a thick tortilla-like favorite of all Africans.

But besides the daily bustle of the streets, there is little else going on in the city. Most people, if they have a few francs, will hang out at some pub and have a few beers with their friends and watch soccer on TV. But that's about it. And every day is pretty much the same.

Maybe this is a perfect situation for revival. When there is not much going on around you to look at, maybe it is time to look up. Certainly the Christians here are hoping for something more than just going to church on Sunday. They want revival; they just don't know what to do.

The pastor of the church where I am preaching was also my host when I was preaching in Ruyigi, so the folks here have heard all about the outpouring of the Spirit that happened in there. So when I walked into the first service, I felt like I was under glass. They were staring at me in hopeful expectations that I would bring the same outpouring here that came down in Ruyigi. Uh, excuse me, but I am not a rainmaker, don't do miracles, and most of the time don't even know what I am doing or how to do it. But I have learned that it is pointless to argue. I represent hope to them, and I dare not take that away.

The first service here did not seem very cohesive to me, but I have been going for several weeks now and am running on empty. There just ain't much left in the bucket to pour out, so it is not surprising to me that I just ain't got it like I had it a few weeks ago.

But then, towards the end of the service, you could feel this shift in the message. I started driving toward salvation, repentance, and having that personal experience and new life with Jesus Christ. I called for them to come to the altar. I could feel it that there were those out there who did not have a right relationship with God, but they were slow to respond.

Then a young girl raised her hand. I told her to come on down. Then another. And another. And then, here they come! Somewhere between 125 to 150 people came down to the altar. Once the flow started, it poured.

I guess it just didn't matter what the message was like. God is dealing with these people. They had come from the town to hear what God had to say and fell like ripe fruit into His hands.

CHAPTER 27
BREAKING OUT IN GITEGI

On the second day at Gitegi, I brought another message of revival for the church and 11 souls got saved during the altar call. For the most part, however, the Lord was dealing with the church to change from their complacency to a vibrant walk of action. If you want revival, you can't just sit there and wait – you have to do something or nothing will happen. And that starts with prayer and repentance. The seed was planted and it bore forth fruit the next evening.

The third service in Gitegi was electrifying from the very start. I knew it would be good because I could feel myself falling back into the free flow of the Spirit. The message just rolled out of me and connected with their hearts. The place was packed with people from all over town, not just this church. When the word spread that the Spirit of God was moving in these services, people came. Just like in Jesus' ministry, when people are hungry for Truth, they will drop everything they are doing and walk a hundred miles to come to Jordan to hear the Word of God.

When I gave the altar call, it was like a mighty river poured out of the pews down to the altar. 250 souls came down – some for first-time salvation, others for re-dedication and repentance for dead works. I say 250, but really, you just had to guess because there were so many that you couldn't count them. What a cry was heard! What a refreshing and a cleansing in the air! What a transformation in the church! And what a promising beginning for revival in this little town of Gitegi!

This was my last service for this campaign. I am more than ready to go home. It is difficult to relay to others the price that is paid to bring this message of revival to these different towns and villages. Money is the most obvious, each trip costing several thousands of dollars, but the invisible costs of the strain of delivering message after message, continued traveling, food, and separation from home are often overlooked. I am tired of eating alone. The real hardships, however, are spiritual in nature. Satan never sleeps and is constantly at work in the spiritual, mental, and emotional realm. The only relief comes when the saints begin to hold up a defense around you in prayer. You can feel the dramatic difference when they break through.

But when you can see the vision spread out before you in the shining faces of these people who have just entered into a new hope that God will really move in their lives, their churches, and their communities, the price diminishes to nothing. What could possibly be more important than this? When I am out here delivering my soul to these hungry people, I feel more alive than ever.

I will be back.

CHAPTER 28
LEAVING BURUNDI

I am writing this to my friends and supporters to update you on what has been happening on this latest trip to Africa. This has been, by far, the most difficult campaign I've had, not only in the intensity of the schedule but in the continuing barrage of attacks by the devil, but this trip has also offered the most hope.

We started in Rwanda and preached at several churches there, both small and large. We immediately noticed that there was a different feel to things there. While they were hungry for the message, it was as if there was a closed door down at the bottom of their hearts that was locked shut. I believe it is because the enormous emotional and spiritual wounds from the Genocide. The depth of the horror is incalculable to us in the West and has caused such deep pain that they have shut up the deeper recesses of their hearts. They need revival desperately.

I was able to reach several churches through seminars, which usually lasts 3 days, in regular church services to whole congregations, and in some daytime luncheon services that are common out here. Before I left, I was invited to preach on the radio on a couple of occasions, one of which was Radio Rwanda that went out to the whole country. I will be back in Rwanda next week to spend 3 more days with another church, this time in one of the other cities.

We flew to Burundi a few weeks ago and have been on a pressing schedule since we arrived, sometimes preaching at two different churches a day. I have spoken to so many places and said so many things to so many people that I don't know what I've said to whom. Sometimes I feel like a robot – get up, go to church, bring the message, back to the hotel, back to church, bring the message again, back to the hotel, back to church, bring the message again… After a while, you begin to feel like you are out of steam and I have to cry out to God for a renewal of passion and feeling. I will have preached at well over 100 services by the time I am done, and that has a mind-numbing effect after a while, especially since the main purpose of my mission is to bring this one message of revival.

In the meantime, we have had things stolen, including all the PA equipment and parts off the car. In Uganda, the police arrested the wife of my associate, Pastor Noah, and threw her and her baby girl into jail – for no reason! All a mistake and finally resolved, but you can imagine the effect it has had on us while we are out here in another country trying to focus on the mission. Back home, anything that can break will break, and a lot of things that cannot break will break anyway. If it can go wrong, it will. Now mind you, all this starts the day I purchase the airplane tickets and continues until I get home. I'm sorry, but this is NOT coincidence.

It is the emotional toll, however, that is the hardest. I liken it to being under a mental and emotional Cyber attack. You really can't pinpoint what it is or where it is coming from, but there is a nebulous cloud of murky oppression that you have to trudge through. It is difficult to explain to someone who has not experienced it, but suffice it to say that it is like slogging through mud. While I am dedicated to the mission and inspired with the vision, I feel spent and uninspired and can't wait to get home.

The results, however, have been incredible. Here in Burundi where I had so much trouble last year, it is as if they have been waiting for me. I have been on national TV, preached at some of the biggest churches, shared the vision with the leaders of some of the big denominations, and given out hundreds of Bibles and booklets. Even the President has my book. This message that I am bringing has been an answer to prayer for many of these churches ... literally. They are desperate for a move of God and they instinctively know that it is not without a price. They just don't know what to do. When I bring this message of the Four Steps to Revival, it is as if someone threw open the curtains to flood the room with sunshine. It literally shatters the glass ceiling over their faith. They get it! They really get it! And they are jumping-up-and-down in excitement because now they know that revival – true revival, not the Prosperity Revival they hear on American TV – is within their grasp. It has now become the substance of things hoped for. Revival is on the way.

There have not been any reportable miracles that I know of on this trip. But then, I am not here to do miracles; I am here to deliver a message. After working so hard for the last 8 years, I am finally seeing things take root and begin to push up out of the ground. I can see the vision coming to focus in their eyes, and the answer cannot be far behind.

I heard a brother comment that he does not send his tithes and offerings outside America, and that we should take care of home first. I disagree. Besides the pointed message in Esther of the reliance between the oppressed church of Mordecai and the blessed church of Esther, there is another dynamic at work that we need to be aware of. Our revival will not start in America but will come to us from Africa.

We will not experience revival until our fallow ground has been broken up. We are too comfortable, and, like the Church of Laodicea, we don't even realize how blind, poor, and miserable we really are. No matter how much we repeat that the Great Awakening is coming, it will not come without a deep, penetrating price. We want revival, but we want a revival of convenience without blood, without tears, and without brokenness. There is no such revival.

Revival will not start in America. It will start in Africa. They are ripe for a move of God. They are dry, desperate, humbled before God and open to hear His Word. True, there is still a ways to go, but they are so much closer than any other place.

America doesn't want revival bad enough to cry out to God for it because our blessings have made us too comfortable with the world. Just as the children of Israel were slaves for 400 years and got used to their slavery, so America has gotten used to the spiritual famine that has entered the Church. God had to raise a Pharaoh who was deadly in his oppression to make the Israelites desperate enough to cry out to God. So also will American have to be brought to a place of brokenness before we will be able to cry out to God in true broken-hearted desperation. Those are the cries that God will hear.

Like a wildfire in a field of dry, parched wheat, however, once the fire starts, it will explode. And it will be so hot that we will feel the heat around the world. I am just planting the seeds for that revival and am striking matches out in the wheat field.

CHAPTER 29
FINAL RESULTS

It's been almost three weeks since I've gotten home. This was the hardest trip I have even been on ... and probably the most important. The attacks we and those who were around us went through were pretty tough – from sickness, theft, and broken vehicles to false imprisonment and false accusations. But the things we accomplished were even greater.

The funny thing is that the most notable accomplishments were not necessarily the most important. I preached for one hour on nationwide TV in Burundi, two separate hours on Radio Rwanda, was a keynote preacher at the biggest church in Burundi on 3 occasions, invited to meet the President, etc.. But these were not the things that I counted as the biggest things we did.

Another blind man got healed, along with several others, including a man with a broken arm. We saw this with our own eyes! But I didn't go there to do miracles.

Somewhere between 400 to 500 souls got saved while I was at each church, and they kept going out to get more after I had left to go to the next church. But I'm not an evangelist who has great big crusades to "bring 'em down to the altar". I'm an arsonist, not an evangelist. My job is to set the churches on fire so that THEY go get them and bring them down to the altar.

The things that were most important were the reactions we got throughout the countryside in the little churches in villages that never see a white man, much less a preacher. We would go to these out-of-the-way places to be met by maybe a dozen people or so. If you don't have a good grip, that can be discouraging to have spent so much money and driven so many miles to come so far ... for a dozen people. But this is what the Lord has for me to do – go to the places that no one else will go and preach His Word.

So you stand up – it doesn't matter how exhausted you are from delivering 2 and 3 messages a day for two months straight – and you hold up the microphone, and BAM! The Holy Ghost falls down out of the sky and you are on a roll for the next hour! It happened like this for 100 services in 60 days. You watch as the church gets transformed before your eyes as Holy Ghost conviction falls on them for "having church" instead of what God called them to do, which is win souls.

Altar calls here are loud, wet, and long. And when they are done, there is a cleanness in the air and a broken freedom that they did not have before. Now, we're ready for revival!

By the time 3 days have past, scores of people (sometimes hundreds) have arrived after having walked on foot for 5 and 6 hours to get here, just so they can sleep on the ground, eat rice and beans, and walk all the way home when it is over. But oh God, is it worth every step they had to take! I'm not talking about great services, neither am I talking about exciting message – I'm talking a supernatural outpouring as the heavens split wide open and the power of God fills the place where we are at. People get healed just by walking into the service! Those places will never be the same again.

It would be one thing if it was just a great time that we had and then it was over. "Had a nice time. Thank you. But we're going back to our normal life now." If that was all it was, then at least we touched the Throne of God. But it isn't. I am still getting messages of how these churches have doubled and tripled in size in just a few weeks. One church is begging my associate Noah to come and teach them how to go out into the streets and witness. Another has taken the message to go out into the city two-by-two and bring in souls. Others are taking the booklet, "Four Steps to Revival" to other churches to share this message of revival with others. I just received a phone call that one pastor had taken it into Southern Sudan and they are begging to hear more. And there is so much more …

All this is because of the folks who support us and back us up in prayer. It just seems so incredible to me that God would use a handful of little people like us to be part of all these really great things that He is doing. Did I say that right? Does that make sense? I'm just a marionette on a string that is held up by the prayers of the saints, but those who spend the time on their knees holding us up are the ones who have sacrificed to make all this happen. Thank God that He has touched your hearts.

I don't know where I'll be going next, but I'm sure the Lord will point me in the direction He wants. And most likely, it will be somewhere remote where nobody else will go.

That's okay. It's the way He always does it, isn't it?

DALEN GARRIS

EPILOGUE:
REPORT ON THE RWANDA AND BURUNDI MISSION

By Pastor Noah Kamanzi

We did Revivalfire conferences in two countries, Burundi and Rwanda. The purpose of these conferences was to bring unity of the body of Christ and to rise together in power to bring a great harvest to the Lord. Because of cultural grievances, these people have not been able to unite together to do anything as one body that represents Christ. Satan used the Genocide that had claimed thousands of souls in this both countries to separate the two tribes, the Hutu and the Tutsi. But Dale, under the anointing of the Holy Spirit, stood out with boldness, and shared the need for revival and the urgency for winning souls, saying that we need to rise above the challenge and go reach out as one body to the lost and dying souls in both countries.

To organize the meetings, we reached out to the leaders in both Burundi and Rwanda, we planned meetings, got permissions from the Government to secure venues, and did publicity on Radio and Television. We sent out invitation letters and SMS messages to as many churches as we could.

Places We Visited:

Rwanda University - This was in the up country where we had 400 to 500 kids. Dale shared about the cost of true revival and gave out a hundreds of *Four Steps to Revival*. The message was received here with such excitement that when we left, the kids began to form reading groups, set up times of prayer for revival, and formed a group called the Gideon Generation. This group has taken this message to all the other universities in Rwanda and has shared the vision with students in Burundi. Out this, hundreds of kids are giving their souls to the Lord. What a great blessing!

Agape Church - This church is near the university where we did a three day seminar of Four Steps to Revival. This church is being led by the Tutsi Pastor whom the Lord has transformed. He has broken the spirit of tribalism, and asked the church to repent of their sins, and because of that, the church has come back to life. Souls are coming to get saved at every service. He wants Dale to go back so that He can share with him about the miracles that are happening in the church.

Kibungo Church - The church has put the message in practice, and as a result have increased in number. They pleaded with me to bring Dale back again. The pastor has invited many leaders and Pastors to hear this message so that their churches can also be revived like his! He does not want to keep these things to himself. Praise the Lord.

If I try to tell you about all the churches, it would take a long time, but let me say that I have gone back to Rwanda and have met all the leaders we visited, and they are all excited.

Bujumbura, Burundi - The six places we visited in Burundi have experienced a great change. The New Vision Church, where we prayed through 300 souls, has instituted two services on Sunday. They have not stopped. They said that they saw it work, so they have started to have an evening crusade every night. They have won so many souls that they had to start a second service to fit everyone in the church.

I would like to take an opportunity to thank Dale and Sister Cindy, plus your friends and donors who gave money so you could come. Thank you for your commitment, your hardworking passion for revival, and your unspeakable heart for souls. We appreciate you for your generous heart! Many people who did not have a Bible, got one and used them to win more souls. The books that we had printed, *Four Steps to Revival*, have painted a clear picture for us to lead people unto repentance and step out to win the lost. Your testimony of how it was like in those early years has also encouraged many people.

And also to thank our all-knowing God, who brought us together in this business of expanding the kingdom of God.

I hope in five years' time Rwanda and Burundi will be turned upside down for this great revival of all the time because of the fire that has caught!!!!!! Praise the Lord!

Final Remarks:

There is still great need for *Four Steps to Revival* to be translated in Kinyarwanda so that all people can get a copy.

Many people who have received the message are on the front lines, taking the message, sharing the vision, and encouraging others to go also. Many are willing to go, but the challenge is a lack of Bibles. They are willing to go out to bring this message, but cannot afford to buy a Bible.

We pray that the Lord will provide the finances for you so that you could do five trips because of the need for revival is so great.

Pastor Noah Kamanzi,
noahkamanzi@yahoo.com

ABOUT THE AUTHOR

Dalen Garris has been in ministry since 1970 during the Jesus Movement in California. In 1997, he started a radio broadcast that was heard on stations around the world for almost 12 years. A newspaper column followed, for which he has written over 700 articles, which were published in newspapers and Christian magazines in several countries. He has also written several books and booklets.

Since 2004, he has been lighting the fires of revival in churches spread across sub-Saharan Africa. During the course of 15 years, he has preached in almost 1,000 churches, has seen hundreds of churches set on fire and explode with growth. He has prayed with hundreds of people who were supernaturally healed and tens of thousands who have been saved. And the fires are still burning.

Because of his work across Africa, Dalen Garris was awarded an honorary Doctorate in 2017 by the Northwestern Christian University of Florida.

Dr. Garris currently lives with Cindy, his wife of 40 years, in Waxahachie and is still heavily involved with churches across Africa. His pressing hope is in seeing this upcoming generation be the Gideon Generation that will usher in this last, great revival that he has preached about for so many years.

RevivalFire Ministries
http://revivalfire.org

RevivalFire Ministries

Please visit our website, http://revivalfire.org, for more information about our ministry. If you or your church would like us to minister, please contact us and we would be more than willing to bring this same message of revival to your group or congregation.

Books by Dalen Garris
Four Steps to Revival
Fire in the Hole
The Kenya Diaries
A Trumpet in Nigeria
A Scent of Rain
Into the Heart of Darkness
Do You Have Eternal Security?

Booklets by Dalen Garris
A Volcano in Cape Verde
Tanzania, 2011
Nigeria, 2012
Planting a Seed in Liberia
A Whisper in the Wind
Finishing What We Started
Two Covenants
Calvinism Critiqued

www.ingramcontent.com/pod-product-compliance
Lightning Source LLC
Chambersburg PA
CBHW050443010526
44118CB00013B/1665